SOCIAL NETWORKING

ABDO
Publishing Company

TECHNOLOGY
PIONEERS

SOCIAL NETWORKING

MYSPACE, FACEBOOK, & TWITTER

by Marcia Amidon Lusted

Content Consultant
Montana Miller, PhD
assistant professor, Department of Popular Culture
Bowling Green State University, Ohio

CREDITS

Published by ABDO Publishing Company, 8000 West 78th Street, Edina, Minnesota 55439. Copyright © 2011 by Abdo Consulting Group, Inc. International copyrights reserved in all countries. No part of this book may be reproduced in any form without written permission from the publisher. The Essential Library™ is a trademark and logo of ABDO Publishing Company.

Printed in the United States of America,
North Mankato, Minnesota
112010
122011

Editor: Mari Kesselring
Copy Editor: Jennifer Anderson
Interior Design and Production: Kazuko Collins
Cover Design: Emily Love

Library of Congress Cataloging-in-Publication Data
Lusted, Marcia Amidon.
  Social networking : Myspace, Facebook, & Twitter / by Marcia Amidon Lusted.
      p. cm. — (Technology pioneers)
  Includes bibliographical references and index.
  ISBN 978-1-61714-811-8
  1. Social networks. I. Title.
  HM742.L87 2011
  302.30285—dc22
                              2010037885

TABLE OF CONTENTS

Facebook is one of the most popular social networking sites.

THE WORLD OF SOCIAL NETWORKING

For millions of Americans today, social networking has become a part of their daily routines. They come home from school or work, turn on their computers, and log onto Facebook, MySpace, or Twitter. From the comfort of home, people can communicate with hundreds of friends at once by posting a status update or a "tweet" on Twitter. On Facebook or MySpace, they read their friends' status updates and wall posts. Maybe they have some great new photos to post and share. They may accept an invitation to "friend" someone. They might send that person a message, especially if they have not talked in a long time. Maybe their classmates are online and they chat on Facebook as they do homework. And those users may not be the only one in their households using social networking. They may have a parent sharing photos with relatives or reconnecting with old college friends.

MySpace and Facebook provide an easy way for people to have their own space on the Internet. Users can set up a profile page with their personal information and photos. They can easily stay in touch with friends—even receiving e-mails or text alerts to their cell phones when someone posts a status update or sends them a message. Unlike Facebook users, MySpace users can also create colorful blogs and send bulletins to their friends. Using editing tools and templates, they can customize their profile pages with colorful backgrounds and music.

THE EVOLUTION OF SOCIAL NETWORKING

Most people mistakenly believe that online networks did not exist before the twenty-first century. However, as far back as the 1980s, people could communicate through electronic bulletin board systems (BBSs). These sites, which were free and operated by computer hobbyists, allowed users to post information and engage in discussions. They usually involved only people who lived in the same area, since connecting to the Internet was done through phone lines and distant users would have to pay long-distance phone rates.

Another early interactive service was CompuServe, which began in the 1970s as a computer-based communication system for businesses. Eventually, Internet providers and search engines such as America Online (AOL), Yahoo, and Google also fostered member sites where users could interact. The first recognizable social network—using the same definition as today's Facebook and MySpace sites—was SixDegrees.com, launched in 1997. It allowed users to make lists of friends, send messages, and construct profiles. SixDegrees went out of business in 2000 but was soon followed by many other social networking sites: LiveJournal in 1999, Friendster in 2002, MySpace in 2003, Facebook in 2004, and Twitter in 2006.

For those who are looking to send information to many people quickly, there is Twitter. Twitter is a form of "microblogging"—that is, the use of very short messages that are limited in size by the system itself. A user who has signed up with Twitter can post and receive messages to an entire network of contacts. Messages are limited to 140 characters. They are intended to be brief status updates or a way to organize a gathering or conduct a group conversation. Twitter posts—known as "tweets"—are text only. However, users can easily post pictures along with their tweets through the "twitpic" feature. They can also include links to other contents in their tweets. As with MySpace and Facebook, users can also choose to receive messages from people in their network, or block them if they become excessive or annoying.

A GROWING WAY TO CONNECT

Social networking Web sites such as Facebook, MySpace, and Twitter have impacted daily life and social relationships in a profound way. They have also raised important questions. Do social networking sites provide positive ways for people to share and stay in touch? Or are they encouraging people to become ever more isolated from one another, as they avoid face-to-face conversation in favor of connecting online? Many fear that social networking sites make users vulnerable to identity theft, threaten privacy, and even expose young people to online predators. Regardless of popular opinion as to their worth, social networking sites have quickly become one of the most popular methods of communication.

According to statistics from 2010, Facebook had more than 500 million active users. MySpace

MySpace users have a list of friends on their profiles.

had more than 122 million. Traffic at the Twitter Web site increased from 2.5 million tweets a day in 2009 to almost 50 million by February 2010. Social networking is now an established part of US popular culture.

BUSINESS OPPORTUNITY

Social networking sites were initially intended for personal interaction, not for business. However, these sites are also lucrative platforms for businesses to market their products and services. Either by placing advertisements on pages or by operating fan sites on

Facebook for products, musical groups, or companies, businesses can accomplish a great deal of advertising while paying less than they do for ads on traditional Web sites, in print, and on television.

As more people join social networking sites, money spent on advertising is going up. On Facebook alone, advertisers spent $305 million in 2008, double the amount they spent in 2007. And yet advertising via social networks can be tricky, as many users dislike the amount of advertising already on these sites. Right now, most advertisements on social networking sites are limited to traditional display ads, which appear on the side of the user's page similar to ads in a magazine. These ads often target the user based on information taken from his or her profile. For example, users who indicate they are single may see ads for dating services,

COMPUSERVE

CompuServe was one of the pioneering sites that allowed the public to network and interact in the way that today's sites do. Technology writer Christopher Nickson described CompuServe's unique role: "CompuServe allowed members to share files and access news and events. But it also offered something few had ever experienced—true interaction. Not only could you send a message to your friend. . . . You could also join any of CompuServe's thousands of discussion forums to yap with thousands of other members on virtually any important subject of the day. These forums proved tremendously popular and paved the way for the modern iterations we know today."[1]

while a user listed as "engaged" might see ads for bridal shops. This practice has upset many users, who object to the idea that social networking sites are selling their personal information for marketing purposes.

SOMETHING FOR EVERYONE

Some smaller social networking sites cater to special interests. Groups may form around common interests and abilities, political views, or a shared ethnic heritage or national identity. Care2.com, for example, helps activists meet and discuss causes they care about. Couchsurfing.org connects travelers to people who can offer them a guestroom, or even just a couch to sleep on, in other parts of the world. MyChurch.org helps Christian church members connect with one another. Sites like these are sometimes referred to as "passion-centric" social networking sites.

SOCIAL NETWORKING STARS

Of all the social networking sites, MySpace, Facebook, and Twitter occupy the top slots when it comes to popularity and use. Who were the minds behind these sites, and how did they evolve from small, localized networks to the social networking giants they are today? The stories of these sites and their creators are stories of success, but also of bitter rivalries, multimillion-dollar business deals, and struggles for control. And it all started with a Web site that called itself, simply, "a place for friends." MySpace appealed to an audience hungry for a new kind of social interaction. +

Twitter allows users to post up-to-the-minute status updates.

Chris DeWolfe came up with the initial idea for MySpace.

FROM FINANCE AND FILM TO MYSPACE

One was a jock who played varsity basketball and tennis. The other was a high school dropout who played in rock bands. They seemed like an odd pair, but Chris DeWolfe and Tom Anderson would work together to create MySpace, one of the most popular social networking sites in the world.

SPARK OF AN IDEA

Chris DeWolfe was born in December 1965 and grew up in Portland, Oregon. Both of his parents were teachers. His father, Fred DeWolfe, was a historian who wrote several books about Portland history. His mother, Brigitte, taught German at a local college. Chris and his brother, Andrew, attended public schools in Portland. As a high school student, Chris was a varsity player in both basketball and tennis and competed in the state tennis championships along with his brother.

Chris graduated from high school in 1984. Although his parents hoped he might follow in their footsteps and become a teacher, Chris was not interested. Instead, he majored in finance at the University of Washington in Seattle. After graduating in 1988, Chris drifted around the San Francisco Bay

PEOPLE, NOT TECHNOLOGY

Chris DeWolfe is not a technical wizard when it comes to Web sites and the Internet. Instead, he relies on finding talented people and building a team, helping them develop their talents and optimize their skills. It was DeWolfe's circle of friends who would ultimately help build MySpace. DeWolfe's own MySpace page states, "I like being around creative people, funny people, crazy people."[1]

In 2000, Tom Anderson met Chris DeWolfe.

area. Pressured by his family to come up with a plan for his life, he enrolled in the University of Southern California's (USC) Marshall School of Business to pursue a master's in business administration.

At USC business school in 1997, DeWolfe took a course that would ultimately lead to the idea for MySpace. The class was called The Impact of Technology on Media and Entertainment. DeWolfe wrote a paper for the class that hinted at what would come later. According to DeWolfe:

> *In one class, I did a paper . . . for a company I called SiteGeist. The whole idea was to have Internet communities in every city, where people could connect around shared interests—whether nightlife or shopping or entertainment—and to have all the communication tools that went along with that, including email and instant messaging.*[2]

Not only did DeWolfe earn a good grade on his paper, but later on he would hire his professor for the class, Paul Bricault, to promote MySpace.

INTO THE REAL WORLD

After graduating from business school in 1997, DeWolfe married Lorraine Hitselberger. The young couple moved to Pasadena, California, where DeWolfe began working for childhood friend Andrew Wiederhorn. DeWolfe ran the credit card division of Wiederhorn's company, Wiltshire Financial Services. DeWolfe's hard work led to increased revenue in that division, but he was bored by the job and weary of the long commute. Meanwhile, the Internet revolution was taking place, and he wanted to be a part of the excitement.

In 1999, DeWolfe left Wiltshire Financial to become head of marketing for a new company called XDrive. At that time, most people could not afford backup storage for their computer files. XDrive provided this service for free, hoping to make money by selling advertising on the site. At its peak, the company employed 300 people. Its offices were so spacious that employees used scooters to get around. DeWolfe supervised 80 people in XDrive's consumer marketing group. Besides marketing their company's services, the group started a newsletter called *IntelligentX* that featured technology news. They hoped to make money by selling advertising in the newsletter.

MEANWHILE, BACK IN ESCONDIDO . . .

Five years younger than DeWolfe, Tom Anderson—who would one day be the other half of the MySpace team—was born in Escondido, California in 1970. His father was an entrepreneur, and according to Anderson, "had one crazy idea after another."[3] By the time Anderson was in high school, he was fascinated by the new world of computers and online bulletin board systems, which were the forerunners of social networking sites. Anderson made friends with several college-age computer hackers. He later had his computer confiscated by the FBI, although he was never arrested for hacking. Eventually, Anderson dropped out of high school and started playing in a rock band called Top Hatt. He also wrote a technical computer software book that was published in 1989.

Anderson eventually returned to school, studying English and rhetoric at the University of California at Berkeley. After graduating in 1998, he moved to San Francisco and played in a rock band called Swank. He spent a few months living in Taiwan before enrolling at the University of California, Los Angeles (UCLA). There, he earned a graduate degree in film studies.

HACKING AROUND

One of Tom Anderson's friends was infamous computer hacker Bill Landreth, known on online bulletin boards as "the Cracker." In 1983, at the age of 16, Landreth was convicted of computer fraud after hacking into the GTE Telemail system, an early e-mail network. Although he did not access anything of value, Landreth was caught at a time when the United States was just beginning to worry about computer fraud. Convicted, he had to pay a fine of $87 and spend three years on probation. Anderson was impressed with Landreth's hacking abilities and looked up to him as a role model. Landreth introduced Anderson to the hacker community.

Bill Gladstone, a literary agent who helped Landreth win a $25,000 contract to write a book on his life as a hacker, remembered meeting Anderson as one of Landreth's friends. He commented that Anderson seemed well dressed and intelligent. "Tom seemed the most normal. Bill and his other friends seemed to be much geekier and more limited in their future options."[4]

THEIR PATHS CROSS

In 2000, Anderson was walking in his neighborhood when he picked up a flyer offering $20 to anyone who answered the ad. In debt and needing money for a planned trip to Singapore, Anderson answered the ad and found himself in a focus group interview, testing products for XDrive. The interviewer was impressed with Anderson and hired him as a copywriter.

Anderson intended to keep the job for just a few weeks to make some quick money. But it was not long before he got DeWolfe's attention. When testing a new product, Anderson was able to explain concisely why the new product was not working from a user's perspective. DeWolfe was so impressed with Anderson that he offered him a job in marketing at XDrive.

Anderson had landed his first corporate job at XDrive. But more importantly, his relationship with DeWolfe would lead him to success and fame as a cofounder of one of the world's biggest social networking sites. +

Anderson and DeWolfe began their partnership as coworkers at XDrive.

DeWolfe bought the MySpace.com domain name
when he was still working for XDrive.

CREATING MYSPACE

By 2001, both DeWolfe and Anderson were working for XDrive, but times were not good for the company. From roughly 1998 to 2000, during what was known as the dot-com bubble, countless new businesses similar to XDrive had been formed to capitalize on the new popularity of the Internet. Most operated on loans from investors, spending money they had not yet earned in hopes that they would eventually make a fortune from advertising and customer fees. These companies required a great deal of money to start, but because of the excitement over dot-com marketing, investors gladly provided money. And, the stocks for these companies rose quickly in value. But as these companies failed to produce profits, their values fell in the stock market, and the dot-com bubble burst. Hundreds of Internet-based companies filed for bankruptcy and went out of business.

After the dot-com bubble burst, advertisers who had previously invested heavily in Internet ads were now looking elsewhere. XDrive suffered from the lack of advertising money.

A NEW WORLD

According to DeWolfe, online networking did not have a good reputation before 2003. "There was sort of a stigma about socializing online. It was kind of creepy, almost desperate. It's like if you met someone on a dating site, it would've been really weird."[1] But he realized that MySpace was going to change that. "I was at a dinner with five people, and two of them went, 'Oh yeah, I'm on MySpace.' That was a pretty big deal for me."[2]

NAMING MYSPACE

In 2001, DeWolfe bought the domain name of a company called MySpace, a competitor to his old company XDrive. The company had actually been one of DeWolfe's first e-mail consulting clients, but in June 2001 the company ran out of money and its Web site ceased to exist. DeWolfe bought the domain name for $5,000, although at the time, he did not even know what he planned to do with it.

Meanwhile, too few customers were signing up for XDrive's storage services.

In February 2001, Karl Klessig was hired by XDrive as their new executive vice president. Klessig was astounded by the size of XDrive's marketing department and the amount of money the company was spending every month. Ultimately, Klessig decided to lay off the entire marketing division, including Anderson and DeWolfe. But even that did not save the company. One year later, XDrive declared bankruptcy.

A NEW VENTURE

DeWolfe and Anderson lost their jobs at a terrible time for anyone working in the dot-com industry. Investors were no longer willing to pour money into new businesses. Most Internet-based companies were cutting employees in order to stay afloat. Despite the unfavorable economic climate, DeWolfe decided to start a new Internet-based venture of his own: ResponseBase. With his emphasis on loyalty and teamwork, DeWolfe hired a start-up team that included several people from XDrive, including Anderson. ResponseBase was a marketing firm that used mass e-mailing—often known as "spam"—as a way to advertise products and services. The company's business methods were questionable, since they sent e-mail ads to people who had not agreed to receive them. Still, they were not as unscrupulous as some companies out there. According to Julia Angwin in *Stealing MySpace*:

> *At this time, the line between spam and legitimate e-mails was still blurry. . . . On one extreme were marketers . . . which legitimately sent out millions of e-mails to customers who had requested them and immediately honored requests to be removed from the list. On the other extreme were off-shore spammers who used stolen e-mail [addresses] and sent millions of unsolicited e-mails. In between the two extremes were tons of marketers for hire whose tactics varied greatly. DeWolfe joined the in-between group.[3]*

The company began by writing marketing newsletters on behalf of clients, which were then e-mailed to potential customers. Soon it was also sending e-mails advertising its own services and had established its own Web site. Since the company had no customer list of its own yet, it used e-mail addresses of former XDrive subscribers, which the XDrive employees had copied and brought with them when they left the company. The company received numerous complaints about unsolicited e-mails, but they continued to send spam to anyone who had once registered with XDrive.

Through these tactics, ResponseBase quickly built a database of more than 30 million e-mail addresses and was consistently making money. The company branched out into selling e-books as well as a special kind of spyware that would enable consumers to spy on other people who used the same computer they did.

Anderson began traveling to China in search of more products to sell online. ResponseBase's revenues grew rapidly. Soon, the company's success attracted the attention of a group called e-Universe, which wanted to buy ResponseBase.

THE BIRTH OF MYSPACE

In September 2002, e-Universe bought ResponseBase. Unfortunately, e-Universe was not a company with a good reputation. It was known as a copycat company, which built cheap imitations of other Web sites. Like ResponseBase, it was known for operating on the fringes of the Internet, with business practices that were not completely honest. It also marketed spyware that was secretly installed on people's computers when they visited certain Web sites or downloaded certain "free" items such as special cursor symbols.

Despite e-Universe's poor reputation, the partnership worked well for a while. By 2003, however, ResponseBase was no longer making as much money for e-Universe. DeWolfe and Anderson began brainstorming new ideas.

SPYWARE

Just what is spyware? Spyware is any software program that is installed on a user's computer without his or her knowledge or consent, with the purpose of "spying" on the user's Internet activity and gathering information valuable to advertisers and other interested groups. Spyware might download when the user clicks on a pop-up window or visits a certain Web site. One of the types of spyware created by the e-Universe company was an application that turned the computer's mouse pointer into an American flag. People who downloaded this special cursor also unknowingly downloaded software that would display pop-up ads whenever they surfed the Internet. The spyware also provided information about the user to advertisers.

They considered several ideas, including a dating Web site and a class reunion site. Ultimately, they decided to launch a Web site that would compete with Friendster.com, a social networking site that had become a hot new trend on the Internet. In an interview, DeWolfe and Anderson described coming up with the idea for MySpace:

> *"Tom has a million ideas, and some of them are pretty good,"* says DeWolfe. *"Some of them are a little wacky. But oh, this one was just a phenomenal idea."*

> *"At a basic level, it's just like email on steroids or something,"* says Anderson. *"You can find everybody, and it's got pictures, and you can talk to a bunch of people at once. It's cool."*[4]

Because of his connections to the music industry, Anderson also wanted the new networking site to be a place where musicians could connect with each other and where users could quickly upload music files to their personal pages. And unlike Friendster, which had begun to erase what they called "fakester" profiles (such as pages created for members' pets or favorite television characters), this new site would have fewer rules. According to Anderson:

On Friendster, if you were a band and you made a profile, they would delete it. . . . If you made a profile for your company or for where you lived or a neighborhood or an idea, you'd get deleted. We recognized from the beginning that we could create profiles for the bands and allow people to use the site any way they wanted to.[5]

DeWolfe and Anderson called their new site MySpace, making use of the domain name DeWolfe had purchased years before from an online storage company. On August 15, 2003, MySpace was launched. DeWolfe sent an e-mail to his boss at e-Universe that afternoon, saying,

FRIENDSTER

Friendster got its start in 2002 when computer programmers Jonathan Abrams and Cris Emmanuel set out to create a safe and easy-to-navigate environment where people could browse each other's profiles online. Here friends and friends-of-friends could meet and interact much more quickly than in real life. By 2003, Friendster had more than 3 million users. As of 2010, the site boasted 115 million registered users and was most popular in Asia.

However, in the United States, Friendster was quickly surpassed by MySpace and Facebook. This was partly because the site operated slowly at first, often taking almost a minute to load a new page. The slow operation limited what the site could do, since adding blogs and other tools that would allow users to make their pages more exciting would tax the system even more. Friendster was also a closed system, limiting people to viewing only the profiles directly linked to them, whereas MySpace users could view any profile at all. Many US users moved to MySpace and Facebook where they had more control and creative options on their profiles.

A PLACE FOR MUSIC

MySpace founder Tom Anderson saw the site as a musician-friendly environment right from the start. In just its first few months, MySpace caught on with musicians and their fans. Two previously unknown British bands, the Arctic Monkeys and Clap Your Hands Say Yeah, credit their success to their fan pages on MySpace. Their pages helped spread their music much more quickly than traditional means such as radio play or live concerts. Even established bands began using MySpace as a place to debut new songs.

"We launched MySpace. It's sort of buggy, but the best way to find the bugs is to let people use it and get feedback."[6] The groundbreaking Web site was officially up and running. +

Well-known British band Arctic Monkeys credits
MySpace with its success.

Anderson and DeWolfe appeared on NBC's *Today* television show in 2006.

MYSPACE MATURES

By January 2005, 10 million registered users were on MySpace. The Internet was no longer a place where people were either producing or consuming content. On MySpace, users could do both.

GROWING PAINS

As MySpace grew in popularity, it experienced its fair share of growing pains. When the lead developer for the site quit, the company faced a big challenge. The developer had built MySpace using a computer programming language called Perl, which no one else in the company knew. The entire site had to be rebuilt using the ColdFusion programming language. The rebuild inadvertently resulted in one of MySpace's most appealing attributes. When the programmers re-created the Web site, they left the Web markup language—the programming code that controls what appears on a page—visible to readers. This allowed MySpace users to modify the code to change colors, fonts, or background images. Users could also decorate their walls with graphics, cutting and pasting directly onto their pages. Leaving the code visible created security holes in the site, which hackers could use to gain access to the site and its users. However, MySpace decided to leave it alone, since users loved the added control.

As users were able to be more creative with their pages, even more people were attracted to the site, especially teenagers. Users could also keep journals and communicate with each other. It was an entirely new world of interaction. It was no longer seen as unusual to befriend someone you had never met in real life. MySpace was changing the way people connected socially. It was the beginning of a new era of communication with a new system of social conduct.

"GET IT OUT FAST, FIX IT LATER"

The MySpace philosophy was "Get It Out Fast, Fix It Later." In other words, its goal was to add new features as quickly as possible, regardless of whether the site was actually prepared to handle the technology. Anderson often worked to fix the site when something went wrong or when it crashed completely. MySpace was still user-driven, and if users did not like a new feature, the developers did not waste time perfecting it. They simply dropped the feature and went on to something different. One developer, Peter Amiri, commented, "We would push [a new feature out before it was ready], and then the site would go down for four hours."[1]

Despite the early glitches, MySpace's popularity continued to increase. However, MySpace's lack of restrictions would lead to worries about its safety.

SAFETY ON MYSPACE

As MySpace became a popular place for teenagers, many worried it would attract sexual predators and pornographers looking to take advantage of young people. As columnist Rebecca Hagelin noted:

> *MySpace.com has quickly become the malt shop for today's teens—but unlike [a physical place], this virtual "hang out" is also frequented by unsavory characters who are after our kids. What most teens see as just a fun place to connect with friends has become a sexual predator's and pornographer's playground.*[2]

Cloaked in the anonymity of cyberspace, sexual predators could easily misrepresent themselves as other teenagers on MySpace, luring young women or men to meet up with them. MySpace did not verify ages on profiles or check for

SPEED AND THE INTERNET

People today take fast Internet for granted, but in 2003, most people in the United States were still using super-slow dial-up connections, accessing the Internet through their phone lines. Broadband connections were just gaining popularity, replacing dial-up connections. The increase in speed with broadband was significant. A picture that might take two to three minutes to upload using dial-up could now be loaded in less than 30 seconds. This changed the Internet dramatically. Previously, most people used the Internet to find information or buy products, but as a result of these faster speeds, they could now upload pictures or music files and share them with friends. The Internet had suddenly become more interactive. The time was ripe for personalized social networking pages.

PRIVACY AND SOCIAL NETWORKING

One of people's biggest fears about social networking sites is loss of privacy. But writer Joel Stein, in his *Time* magazine article "You Are Not My Friend," argues that social networking sites are not about privacy. "They're a platform for self-branding. We're not sharing things we don't want other people to know. We're showing you our best posed, retouched photos. We're listing the . . . books we want you to think we've read all the way through. We're allowing other people to write whatever they want about us on our walls, unless we don't like it, in which case we just erase it."[3]

registered sexual offenders, so it was difficult to identify and weed out these abusers. The danger was real, although some experts noted that online sexual predators were rarer than most people believe, and that the problem had been hyped up by the media. To avoid falling victim to an Internet predator, people were urged not to give out personal information or respond to attention from users they did not know.

Meanwhile, pornographers began using MySpace either to solicit business, showcase porn stars, or to attract aspiring models and actors. MySpace prohibited users from posting obscene or lewd content such as nude photos. However, because users could upload photos to their pages immediately, it often took several days for MySpace to identify obscene photos and remove them. Teenagers often posted

Parry Aftab, executive director of WiredSafety.com

inappropriate photos, not realizing that the material could be used against them by future employers or during the college admissions process. Issues such as these led to increasing controversy as to whether teenagers should be allowed to access MySpace or any social networking site.

MySpace responded to concerns about the safety and appropriateness of the site by taking steps to prevent predators from getting on the site in the first place. In 2005, MySpace started working with Internet safety organizations such as WiredSafety.org. By 2006, MySpace had changed the site so that users 18 or older had to know the full name or e-mail address of a user under 18 in order to add that person as a friend. This was intended to make it more difficult for predators to contact underage people on MySpace. However, with no way to verify ages, people could easily lie about their age and bypass this restriction. MySpace and other social networking sites continue to debate whether it is possible to reliably verify the ages of users.

SELLING MYSPACE

Despite these serious issues, MySpace's popularity continued to surge. Other corporations became interested in buying MySpace. In July 2005, MySpace's parent company e-Universe, which had been renamed Intermix Media, was purchased by News Corporation, a media company owned by mogul Rupert Murdoch, for $580 million. Although some industry analysts predicted that the corporate buyout would turn off users, MySpace continued to grow, with 50 million users in 2006 and 170,000 new users signing up daily.

However, by 2008, the popularity of MySpace had stalled. According to Anderson in an interview with *The Guardian* newspaper, "We felt like we'd peaked. We weren't trailing off but our growth was slowing down. Everyone who was going to get on MySpace got on it long ago."[4] MySpace was now being surpassed by other social networking sites.

In an attempt to stay current, MySpace has continued to launch new ventures and new features such as MySpace Music, where listeners can download music for free. Developers have considered allowing users to export their profiles to interact with non-social networking sites such as Flixster, where people can review movies. However, MySpace continued to struggle. In 2009, DeWolfe stepped down from his position

WHAT'S NEXT FOR CHRIS DEWOLFE?

Since his departure from MySpace in 2009, it was rumored that founder DeWolfe may be starting a new online venture with social gaming. Social gaming refers to a strategy or role-playing game that takes place through a social platform such as MySpace or Facebook and involves multiple players, usually playing with an avatar, or online identity. Popular examples of online social gaming include Farmville on Facebook and Gangsta on MySpace.

Companies such as Zynga and Social Gaming Network have launched games such as Zyngapoker and Warbook. On these sites, instead of competing against a gamer they do not know, social gamers can also compete against family and friends online. These games have become some of the most popular applications on social networking sites.

as chief executive officer of MySpace, although he would continue to act as an advisor. In June 2009, MySpace cut approximately 30 percent of its employees in an attempt to reduce costs.

Things were definitely changing for MySpace. Only two years earlier, Murdoch had dismissed Facebook, claiming it was not much more than a Web version of a phone book, whereas MySpace was an entire social network where people could connect and live their lives online. But critics complained that MySpace had left itself vulnerable to sexual predators, cyberbullies, spammers, and others with bad intentions. Also, because MySpace allowed its users so many options to personalize their profiles, pages on the site were often chaotic and difficult to navigate. People began seeking online communities with cleaner, user-friendly templates. They found Facebook. +

DeWolfe left MySpace in 2009.

Mark Zuckerberg created Facebook.

CONTROVERSIAL
BEGINNINGS

The most popular social networking site on the
Internet—and as of 2010 one of the five most-
visited Web sites in the world—got its start in a
Harvard University dormitory room late one night in
2003. Mark Zuckerberg, a sophomore, had just been

jilted by a girl he liked. He sat down at his computer and wrote an entry in his blog. "I need to think of something to take my mind off her," Zuckerberg wrote. "I need to think of something to occupy my mind. Easy enough, now I just need an idea."[1] His idea would ultimately lead to the birth of Facebook.

FROM GEEK TO RENEGADE

Mark Zuckerberg was born in White Plains, New York, on May 14, 1984, the son of a dentist, Edward, and a psychiatrist, Karen. Mark received his first computer when he was in middle school and started developing computer programs for gaming and communication. He attended Ardsley High School in New York before moving to Phillips Exeter Academy, a private preparatory school in Exeter, New Hampshire. There, Zuckerberg created several computer programs, including one that helped workers in his father's office communicate. Zuckerberg enjoyed such projects. He and his roommate, Adam D'Angelo, even wrote the software for an MP3 player that could track its users' listening habits and then create a digital music library based on those preferences. This program, called Synapse, was posted on the Web as a free download. Several companies, including AOL, became interested in the program. They approached Zuckerberg, but he refused to sell it.

Zuckerberg was one of the most advanced computer programming students in the school. By the end of his senior year, both Microsoft and AOL offered Zuckerberg impressive salaries to work for their companies. He decided to complete his education before starting a career. After graduating with academic honors from Phillips Exeter, the already successful student enrolled at Harvard University in the fall of 2002.

At Harvard, Zuckerberg continued to experiment with programming projects. In his sophomore year, he built a Web site called Coursematch.com, which allowed students to register for courses online and see who else was registering for those same classes. The site went down when Zuckerberg's laptop, which he used to run the site, crashed from the heavy volume of users. The experience demonstrated to him the popularity of social interaction online, and he realized that computer programming was not just about writing code—it was about understanding people and the things they liked to do. So, Zuckerberg decided to major in psychology instead of computer science.

THE FACEBOOK TRADITION

Prep schools and colleges have a longstanding tradition of publishing annual student directories, complete with photographs. Known as "facebooks," these directories are meant to help students, faculty, and staff get to know each other. As Mark Zuckerberg sat in his dorm room that night in 2003, he had the facebook for his dormitory open on the table next to him. He decided to use women's photos from the facebook (which were available online to dormitory residents) and set up a Web site inviting people to rate their attractiveness. Zuckerberg hacked into the online facebooks for each of the Harvard residence halls, using students' photos without their permission.

Facemash.com was born. Zuckerberg forwarded the link to some of his friends for feedback. By the

FACEMASH CONTROVERSY

Zuckerberg's first online social networking attempt, Facemash, was a way for people to rate women according to their looks. It was similar to a popular Web site called Hot or Not, which allowed visitors to rate the attractiveness of ordinary people based on the photos they submitted to the site. On Facemash, photos of female Harvard students appeared two at a time, and viewers were asked to choose which woman was "hotter." However, the women Zuckerberg included in Facemash had not asked to have their photographs rated, and the site created an outrage. Zuckerberg claimed he did not anticipate the strong negative reaction Harvard women would have to the site.

next morning, more than 450 students had signed up and the page had logged 22,000 views. In just a few hours, however, the Harvard administration had tracked down Zuckerberg and shut down his Internet access. He was called before the university's administrative board and accused of violating student privacy and downloading school property without permission. According to an article in the *Harvard Crimson* newspaper:

> *Zuckerberg said that he was aware of the shortcomings of his site, and that he had not intended it to be seen by such a large number of students. . . . "I wanted some more time to think about whether or not this was really appropriate to release to the Harvard community." After taking it down, Zuckerberg decided that criticism of the site was too strong to re-post it.*[2]

Despite being reprimanded by Harvard, Zuckerberg was now a minor campus celebrity. He also figured out that people were more interested in voyeurism than he had realized. Facemash.com was just the first step to creating a social networking site that would allow people to look into each other's private lives online.

FACEBOOK IS BORN

With the help of several friends at Harvard—Zuckerberg's roommate Dustin Moskovitz and fellow students Chris Hughes and Eduardo Saverin—Zuckerberg began working on a new site, TheFacebook.com, that would ultimately go beyond Harvard and include other schools as well.

Zuckerberg and Saverin each invested money to incorporate the site, with Zuckerberg owning two-thirds of the company. Hughes acted as spokesperson, while Moskovitz helped launch the new site at Stanford, Columbia, and Yale universities. Zuckerberg also enlisted the help of his high school programming partner, D'Angelo, to help set up databases for the growing site.

A STOLEN IDEA?

Ten months before Facebook launched, Divya Narendra and two of his dorm-mates had the idea to create an online community for Harvard students. Beginning in 2003, they worked on coding for the site, but by fall it still was not done. After hearing about the quick rise and fall of Facemash.com, Narendra contacted Zuckerberg, asking him to do some programming for the site in exchange for a part in the company.

Zuckerberg agreed, but over the next few months he did little actual work for the new site. Even though he had assured Narendra that most of the coding for the site was finished, in January he told Narendra to hire a new programmer. While Narendra and his friends did eventually launch their own site, ConnectU, it never took off. They claim that Zuckerberg stole their idea and deliberately delayed the launch of ConnectU in order to launch Facebook first.

TheFacebook officially launched on February 4, 2004. In the first two weeks, 4,000 people signed up. By May 2004, the site had spread at an incredible rate, with more than 200,000 users at 30 different schools.

In a *Harvard Crimson* article, Alan Tabak wrote about the site's immediate popularity:

> *Harvard students are rediscovering the meaning of friendship. An online site designed to connect old and new friends has everyone talking—and typing. . . . Aaron D. Chadbourne '06, said he particularly liked how the website allowed him to see how people in the Harvard community are connected. "I think that's one of the great things about thefacebook.com—that it fosters a sense of community. . . ." [he said.][3]*

TheFacebook was launched, and it was enjoying popularity as the latest, greatest thing. But would it be able to maintain that popularity? +

FACEBOOK: THE MOVIE

In 2010, Columbia Pictures released a movie about the origins of Facebook, entitled *The Social Network*. The film, based on the book *The Accidental Billionaires* by Ben Mezrich, portrays Mark Zuckerberg in a negative light. Filmmakers hoped it would appeal to a wide audience of viewers whether they are on Facebook or not.

[thefacebook]

home   search   global   social net   invite   faq   logout

[My Friends]

[export]

[global]

Export contact informa
in Outlook and other

[invite]

riends to join thefacebook.

Find friends at other schools.

Friends

[Recently Updated Profiles]   [Other Schools]   [GWU]   [All]

Filter:

You have 247 friends.

[message]   [rem

KIP ABER
profile updated recently

[message]   [

Steph Adams

TheFacebook launched in 2004.

Dustin Moskovitz moved to Palo Alto, California, with Zuckerberg.

FACEBOOK MOVES OFF CAMPUS

In the beginning, TheFacebook had a quality that set it apart from other social networking sites. Only users who had an e-mail address from one of the elite schools included in TheFacebook network could join. This created a community of trust, because users had to register as themselves—they could not create anonymous identities. The site was also easy to use. Jeff Jarvis, director of the interactive journalism program at the City University of New York, noted, "It was better than its predecessors. Friendster was a game; MySpace was a tacky home page. Facebook was the best to come along."[1]

The immediate success of TheFacebook.com convinced Zuckerberg to leave Harvard and work for the site full-time. In the summer of 2004, he moved to Palo Alto, California, feeling that Silicon Valley was the best place for a start-up computer company. He originally intended just to take a semester off from Harvard while he took TheFacebook to the next level. He and Saverin agreed to invest another $20,000 each in the company. Saverin came from a wealthy family and did not have a problem investing $20,000. However, Saverin would later claim that

SILICON VALLEY

Silicon Valley is the nickname of the southern San Francisco Bay area in California. The name originally referred to companies in the area that produced silicon microchips for the computer industry. Over time, Silicon Valley became known as a main hub for high-tech companies of all kinds. Venture capital groups, eager to invest money in new technology, sank millions of dollars into local companies. Before the dot-com bubble burst, Silicon Valley and the nearby area had the highest real estate prices in the world. It is still seen as a center for high-tech research and development.

Zuckerberg never contributed his own $20,000 of the investment.

In the house in Palo Alto, Moskovitz, two interns, and other programmers involved in TheFacebook project joined Zuckerberg. They all shared the rent. They spent the summer in front of their computers. They mapped code with bright magic markers on whiteboards, and littered their floors with empty pizza boxes and computer cartons.

Stephen Haggerty, one of Zuckerberg's interns, said, "To call Facebook a company at that point was generous . . . Did we do anything else besides sit in front of our computers? Mark had a girlfriend, but after a while she wasn't around."[2] They were all committed to developing their online social network, rather than pursuing their own social relationships.

MEETING THE NAPSTER

Sean Parker was known for creating the Web site Napster, where users could share music files. Parker learned about a Web site called TheFacebook.com from his girlfriend. Intrigued, he arranged to meet Zuckerberg and Saverin in New York in spring of 2004. At dinner, the three talked about how Parker had raised money for his site in California.

Eventually they became good friends, and Parker moved into the house the Facebook team was renting. Parker introduced Zuckerberg to investors in Silicon Valley. Zuckerberg, however, refused any offers to buy TheFacebook.com.

LAWSUITS AND POPULARITY

At the same time, Zuckerberg and Saverin had a falling-out. Saverin was the business leader of TheFacebook, but he had very little to do with the actual daily workings of the site. He stayed in New York, while the site operated out in California. In 2004, Saverin froze TheFacebook's bank accounts, arguing that it was his money that had provided the start-up funds and that Zuckerberg had never matched those funds as he was supposed to. Saverin also claimed that Zuckerberg had been wrongly using TheFacebook's funds for his personal expenses. Zuckerberg filed a lawsuit against Saverin

SEAN PARKER

Sean Parker, born in 1979, is best known as the cocreator of Napster, an online music file-sharing site. Napster, which operated from 1999 to 2001, allowed users to share their MP3 files with each other for free, making it unnecessary to purchase music through traditional markets. Napster became the object of copyright infringement accusations and lawsuits by the music industry and was shut down by court order in July 2001. It converted to a subscription service, which drastically decreased traffic to the site. The Best Buy Company purchased Napster in 2008.

in order to regain control over the funds, but Saverin countersued.

Because of the suits, Zuckerberg transferred TheFacebook property rights and membership interests to a new version of the company in Delaware. By reorganizing the company and making himself director, Zuckerberg limited Saverin's power and made his shares in the company less valuable. Saverin was no longer considered to be an employee of TheFacebook. In court, Saverin and Zuckerberg eventually reached a settlement, the terms of which were not made public.

In 2005, the company purchased the domain name Facebook.com and dropped "the" from its name. By the spring of 2005, Facebook was more popular than ever. Zuckerberg appointed Parker president of the company, hoping that

THE CONNECTU LAWSUIT

On September 2, 2004, Divya Narendra and twin brothers Cameron S. H. Winklevoss and Tyler O. H. Winklevoss, the founders of the Harvard social networking site ConnectU, also filed a lawsuit against Zuckerberg. They claimed that Zuckerberg stole their idea when he created Facebook. ConnectU also claimed that Zuckerberg delayed his programming work for ConnectU in order to launch Facebook first and failed to meet the conditions of his contract with ConnectU.

The first court case was dismissed in 2007 with no decision reached, but then refiled. The second court case led to a settlement in June 2008, with Facebook buying ConnectU for a reported $65 million in cash and stocks.

Parker's Silicon Valley connections would help him raise investment money for Facebook. However, Parker stayed with the company for less than a year. By that time, Facebook no longer needed Parker's connections in order to attract potential investors. Facebook had already attracted investment dollars. In spring of 2005, one venture capital firm invested $12.7 million in Facebook.

By the end of 2005, Facebook had more than 5.5 million active users. The site had gone beyond college users, expanding to include high school and international school students. Features such as user photo albums had been added. During 2006, Facebook expanded again to include professional networks, now reaching 12 million active users. Advertising banners brought increased revenue, and as more investment money flowed in, Zuckerberg found himself one of the wealthiest 21-year-olds in the world. As of 2010, he had never returned to Harvard to complete his education.

BEACON CONTROVERSY

Zuckerberg continued to look for new ways to make Facebook more than just a social networking vehicle. He saw it as a prime tool for advertisers. On

FACEBOOK RUINS CHRISTMAS

The political activist group MoveOn.org waged a campaign against Facebook's Beacon application. They claimed that not only had Facebook violated its users' privacy by publicizing their buying habits, but it had also "ruined Christmas" for people who shopped online and then found their entire Christmas gift purchase list displayed for their families and friends to see. One user commented, "I saw my [girlfriend] bought an item I had been saying I wanted . . . so now part of my Christmas gift has been ruined. Facebook is ruining Christmas!"[4]

November 2, 2007, he unveiled a new Facebook program called Beacon, which would help online businesses advertise themselves on users' Facebook pages. If a user made a purchase online, the purchase information would show up on the shopper's Facebook page as well as on the shopper's friends' pages. Beacon would also allow someone to post something for sale on a site such as eBay, automatically letting the seller's Facebook friends know what he or she had for sale. According to Zuckerberg, "Nothing influences people more than a recommendation from a trusted friend. A trusted referral influences people more than a broadcast message."[3]

Unfortunately, there was no way for users to opt out of Beacon. Facebook users were surprised when Facebook started tracking their online purchases. Many were

ConnectU founders filed a lawsuit against Zuckerberg in 2004.
It was finally settled in 2008.

outraged over this invasion of privacy. The negative
response was so strong that Zuckerberg apologized in
a message on his Facebook blog:

> *The problem with our initial approach of making
> [Beacon] an opt-out system instead of opt-in
> was that if someone forgot to decline to share
> something, Beacon still went ahead and shared it
> with their friends. It took us too long after people
> started contacting us to change the product so that
> users had to explicitly approve what they wanted
> to share.[5]*

Beacon was changed to an optional utility, so that people's Internet browsing and buying habits were only shared with their friends if they specifically wanted them to be. The Beacon debacle did not slow Facebook down at all, though. The site now had more than 50 million active users and had attracted the interest of one of the biggest computing companies in existence: Microsoft. +

Sean Parker served as president of Facebook for less than a year.

Facebook headquarters are located in Palo Alto, California.

FACEBOOK ALL GROWN UP

In 2008, *Forbes* magazine listed Zuckerberg as a member of its billionaires' club. His worth was estimated at $1.5 billion, which made him the youngest billionaire on the planet at that time. In October 2007, after a public bidding war with

Google, Microsoft Corporation had made a $240 million investment in Facebook, giving Microsoft a 1.6 percent share in it. At that time, Facebook was valued at $15 billion, which many analysts considered an unrealistic figure for a company that had made only $150 million in revenues in 2006. One analyst commented:

> *On the surface it seems insane. Why would Microsoft pay so much for such a small piece of a company? But whether it was $1 billion or $15 billion, it doesn't matter. By making it $15 billion, it assures that no one would come near it. The only one who could buy it now is Microsoft.*[1]

LINGERING PROBLEMS

Even with such a large infusion of cash from Microsoft, Facebook and Zuckerberg were still plagued by problems. Zuckerberg was suffering from a tarnished image, as he was accused of having stolen the idea of Facebook from ConnectU at Harvard. It was difficult to prove that he had committed any crime. After all, it was possible for the same ideas to be generated by two different people at the same time, especially with Harvard's own version of a facebook already functioning as an online campus database. However, the allegations made some businesspeople wary about going into business with Zuckerberg. In 2008, Kara Swisher, a columnist for the *Wall Street Journal*, noted, "He's young—and I'm nervous about that. How many people has he burned, and he's only 24?"[2]

Despite continuing legal troubles, Facebook continued to grow quickly. In 2007, it launched Facebook Ads. This program allowed advertisers to create Facebook pages for their brands, access information about Facebook users and their preferences, and run ads targeted at specific users. Then, in 2008, Facebook co-sponsored the US presidential election debates with ABC News. Also that year, Facebook added a translation application that would enable Spanish, French, German, and 21 other languages to be used on the site. As of 2010, Facebook supported 74 languages.

BLOCKING FACEBOOK

In several countries around the world, including Syria, Iran, China, and Vietnam, access to Facebook is often blocked, as the site allows people to freely criticize their government or other authorities. In some places, antigovernment groups have used Facebook to organize and to communicate with each other. During an election in Iran in 2009, the site was temporarily blocked because of fears that it was being used to organize a radical opposition group.

USER CONTROL

As the site added applications, however, it often received negative feedback from its users. As S. Shyam Sundar, codirector of the Media Effects Research Laboratory at Pennsylvania State University, commented:

> *This is a technology that has inherently generated community, and it has gotten to the point where members of that community feel not only vested but empowered to challenge the company.*[3]

Facebook users tend to feel they should have control over the way the site looks and operates. When Facebook implements new features that users dislike, groups often form to protest the changes. However, Facebook rarely makes changes based on user feedback. "It's not a democracy," Facebook vice president Chris Cox said.

USERS TAKE BACK CONTROL

In 2009, Facebook issued new Terms of Service, in which the company stated that it owned all content on the site. This meant that Facebook could use anything a user put on the site, such as photos or writing, and copy or distribute it in any form they wanted, even after the user had terminated his or her Facebook account. User Julius Harper created a group called "People Against the New Terms of Service." Soon he had 20,000 users enrolled in the group and was getting national media attention. As a result, Facebook reinstated the former Terms of Service and allowed users to vote on a new version. Today the site's Terms of Service give the users rights to all their own original content. Users can control how and where their information can be shared.

"We are here to build an Internet medium for communicating and we think we have enough perspective to do that and be caretakers of that vision."[4]

MAKING MONEY, SPENDING MONEY

Although Facebook has continued to grow, with more than 500 million active users as of 2010, Facebook's revenues have not grown as quickly. While the company does not announce its earnings, analysts estimate that it earned between $700 and $800 million in 2009, which may not have been enough to cover its expenses. Based on these earnings, Facebook is probably worth significantly less than the value of $15 billion claimed by Microsoft.

The reason for Facebook's lack of revenue is one shared by most popular, free online services. Such sites are set up to make money through advertising, but in reality, people rarely click on the ads that appear on these sites. They object to seeing intrusive advertising mixed in with their personal conversations. Facebook has attempted to overcome this problem with a new series of "engagement" ads. These ads invite Facebook users to become fans of

Chris Cox is the vice president of Facebook.

certain products or companies, often in exchange for a discount. If one user becomes a fan, word goes out to all of his or her Facebook friends. Facebook's chief operating officer Sheryl Sandberg says, "We're trying to provide the antidote for the consumer rebellion against interruptive advertising."[5]

Sandberg denied the rumor that Facebook was considering charging its users for use of the Facebook site. As of 2010, she claimed that Facebook's revenue through advertising was growing.

WHO IS USING FACEBOOK?

As Facebook continues to add users, it is important to note just who is using this social networking site. MySpace is still seen as being largely the domain of teenagers, but as Facebook has grown, the median age of its users has increased as well. Between June 2008 and January 2009, Facebook users in the 35 to 54 age group increased from 7 percent to 16 percent of the total number of users, while those in the 18 to 24 age range have seen their percentage fall from 53 percent to 40 percent. There has also been an increase in users aged 55 and older. It appears that Facebook is no longer primarily a place for the socializing of teenagers and those in their twenties. Older people are joining Facebook to reconnect with old friends and classmates.

The challenge for the site is in adjusting its advertising approach to appeal to users both young and old. According to the article "Fogeys Flock to Facebook," which appeared in *Business Week* magazine:

> *The question now for Facebook, marketers looking to advertise there, companies that want to own it, and investors who eventually may buy its shares is whether . . . CEO Mark Zuckerberg and his deputies can keep attracting the [older] crowd while preserving the site's spring-break atmosphere . . .*[6]

LOOKING FOR SOMETHING NEW

Social networking is all about the next new thing, and despite its continuing popularity, in 2006, Facebook saw competition from a newer method of online

FUTURE FOR THE FOUNDERS

Whatever happened to some of the other people who helped start Facebook? Chris Hughes served as the director of online organizing for Barack Obama's presidential campaign in 2008. As of 2010, he worked for a Cambridge, Massachusetts, venture capital firm, General Catalyst Partners. He was also an advisor for GMMB, a political consulting company. In April 2009, Hughes was featured on the cover of *Fast Company* magazine as "The Kid Who Made Obama President: How Facebook Cofounder Chris Hughes Unleashed Barack's Base—and Changed Politics and Marketing Forever."

Dustin Moskovitz left Facebook in 2008 to start a company called Asana, which focuses on creating online methods and software that businesses can use to work together and develop ideas. Eduardo Saverin won the right to be recognized as the cofounder of Facebook but is no longer affiliated with the company. However, he is reportedly worth $1.1 billion due to his Facebook stock.

communication. This new form of social networking was quick, simple, and did not require shuffling through profile updates and messages. Its name was Twitter. +

Some users are dissatisfied with Facebook's privacy settings.

Jack Dorsey's experience with dispatchers gave him the idea for Twitter.

HATCHING TWITTER

For some people who either preferred quick messages or wanted mobile access, connecting with friends by Facebook or MySpace or by regular e-mail was not practical in 2006. The time was ripe for the birth of Twitter. This service allowed users to share their status—what they were doing at a given moment—simply and easily, in just 140 characters of type.

INCUBATING TWITTER

Twitter has its roots in instant messaging and SMS (Short Messaging Service), or texting, on cell phones. Instant messaging allows people who are online at the same time to communicate instantly by typing and sending messages. Texting does not require anyone to be online. But Twitter would take instant messaging and texting a step beyond. With Twitter, messages could be shared with hundreds of friends at once, and displayed on the Internet for all to see.

Jack Dorsey, creator of Twitter, was born on November 19, 1976. He grew up in St. Louis, Missouri. As a teenager, he became

WHY 140 CHARACTERS?

Most cell phones using instant messaging technology are limited to 160 characters before the message is split into two parts. In order to make it easier to send and receive Twitter messages by cell phone, the creators decided to work with this limitation. They allowed 20 characters for the username, which left 140 characters for the message content. This space limitation has inspired some writers to write Twitter novels, either by sharing a story bit by bit in 140-character chunks or by creating ministories that start and finish within 140 characters. The following mysterious tale, written by Ron Gould, won first place in Copyblogger's Twitter Writing Contest:

"'Time travel works!' the note read. 'However you can only travel to the past and one-way.' I recognized my own handwriting and felt a chill. "[1]

interested in dispatch routing, the process by which drivers of delivery trucks, emergency vehicles, taxicabs, and so on are dispatched, or sent, to various locations. He liked how communications from the drivers to the dispatcher were stripped down to the bare essentials: where they were and what they were doing.

At age 14, Dorsey started developing software for a dispatch company in St. Louis. He attended Bishop Dubourg High School in St. Louis and went on to the Missouri University of Science and Technology. After graduation, Dorsey went to New York University. However, in 1995, he dropped out and started work on creating computer programs for DMS, one of the biggest courier services in the country. Eventually, he moved to California.

Dorsey started a company in Oakland, California, in 2000 that would dispatch couriers, taxis, and emergency vehicles via the Internet. Ultimately, his interest in dispatching led him to the idea that would become Twitter. Dorsey says:

> It started with a fascination with cities and how they work, and what's going on in them right now. That led me to . . . bicycle messengers and truck couriers roaming about, delivering packages. . . .

Dorsey turned to Biz Stone, *left*, and Evan Williams at
ODEO to help develop Twitter.

*Then we started adding the next element, which
are taxicabs. . . . And then you get the emergency
services: ambulances, fire trucks, and police—and
suddenly you have this very rich sense of what's
happening right now in the city. But it's missing
the public. It's missing regular people. And that's
where Twitter came in.*[2]

Dorsey's first experiments with sharing his
status in real time with his friends was done through

an RIM 850, a device that was the predecessor to today's Blackberry. He developed a program that allowed him to create a message and send it to an e-mail service that immediately sent it to all of his friends. However, the problem was that if his friends did not have the same RIM 850 device, they could read and respond to the message only if they were at a computer with a keyboard. There was no way to have a back-and-forth exchange. And, if his friends read the message hours later, they no longer had an accurate status for him. Dorsey put the idea aside, but it lingered in the back of his mind.

WHAT'S IN A NAME?

How did Twitter get its name? Dorsey explained the process:

[W]e wanted to capture that feeling: the physical sensation that you're buzzing your friend's pocket. It's like buzzing all over the world. . . . [w]e came up with the word "twitch," because the phone kind of vibrates when it moves. But "twitch" is not a good product name because it doesn't bring up the right imagery. So we looked in the dictionary for words around it, and we came across the word "twitter," and it was just perfect. The definition was "a short burst of inconsequential information," and "chirps from birds." And that's exactly what the product was. The whole bird thing: bird chirps sound meaningless to us, but meaning is applied by other birds. The same is true of Twitter: a lot of messages can be seen as completely useless and meaningless, but it's entirely dependent on the recipient. So we just fell in love with the word. . . . We can use it as a verb, as a noun, it fits with so many other words. If you get too many messages you're "twitterpated"—the name was just perfect.[3]

ODEO, INC.

In 2006, Dorsey approached a podcasting company in San Francisco called ODEO. ODEO was also interested in text messaging and real-time status communication. ODEO founder Evan Williams and employee Biz Stone would help him develop Twitter.

ODEO frequently held daylong meetings during which employees brainstormed about new ideas for the company. The company was not doing well and needed to break its creative slump. Dom Sagolla, another employee, remembers the meeting at which Dorsey talked about the idea that would lead to Twitter:

> *"I want to have a dispatch service that connects us on our phones using text," [Jack said]. His idea was to make it so simple that you don't even think about what you're doing, you just type something and send it. Later [Jack's] idea was selected for prototyping. The first version . . . was entirely web-based. It was created on March 21, 2006. My first [real] message is #38: oh this is going to be addictive.*[4]

The first version of Twitter was limited to ODEO employees and their families. Every user could be monitored on one administrative page so that the company could watch for opinions or issues from their users. At this point the service was called Status/Stat.us. After brainstorming, the name Twitter was born. In July 2006, a full-scale version of Twitter was launched, although it was still limited to individuals and not companies.

However, ODEO was in trouble and its revenues were falling. A few months after launching Twitter, Dorsey, Stone, and Williams founded their own company, Obvious Corporation. They bought ODEO and all its assets, including Twitter. In 2007, Twitter was spun off as its own company. The three men raised millions in funding from venture capital firms. Twitter was ready for wide-scale adoption.

A GROWING FLOCK

Sagolla admits that at first, not many people understood or used Twitter. He explained:

> Very few people understood its value. At that time most people were still paying per [text messages sent from cell phones], and so wouldn't [Twitter] run up our bills? Also, how were we supposed to use this thing and who cares what I'm doing?[5]

Soon, however, people began warming up to Twitter. A landmark moment occurred during the

2007 South by Southwest Festival
(a film and music festival that takes
place every year in Texas), when
Twitter's creators placed two large
plasma screens in the conference's
hallways, streaming only Twitter
messages. Conference attendees
began to keep tabs on each other
with constant Twitter messages.
Soon everyone was talking about
this new messaging service. Tweets
went from 20,000 per day to
60,000.

During a 2007 earthquake
in California, Twitter was used
to share information much more
quickly than broadcast news
services and government agencies,
as people communicated about
where they were and what was
going on. During the 2008
presidential elections, Twitter
users stayed informed about
results and Twitter updates were
even streamed onscreen during
television broadcasts. When US

NOT A SOCIAL NETWORK

Twitter's creators are quick
to point out that Twitter
is really not a social network
such as MySpace or Facebook.
There is none of the social
pressure that comes with
deciding whether or not to call
someone a "friend" or include
relatives in your social network. Users can choose their
level of privacy; they decide
who can view their posts.
They may choose to make their
posts visible only to friends. If
not, the posts will appear for
anyone to see and can also be
accessed by Internet search
engines.

Airways Flight 1549 made an emergency landing in the Hudson River in New York City in January 2009, the first news reports reached the world through a message and image posted to Twitter from someone's cell phone: "There's a plane in the Hudson, I'm on the ferry going to pick up the people. Crazy."[6]

Twitter had entered the mainstream. It began gaining popularity around the world and was sometimes described as the "SMS of the Internet" because it was essentially instant messaging on a large scale. It would not be long before businesses and marketers found ways to use this simple service. Twitter began to expand. +

Twitter users can post messages using computers or cell phones.

From left to right, Evan Williams, Biz Stone, and Jack Dorsey were honored at *Time*'s 100 Most Influential People in the World Gala in 2009.

TWITTER TODAY

In 2009, *Time* magazine listed the three founders of Twitter—Jack Dorsey, Biz Stone, and Evan Williams—among their 100 Most Influential People in the World. Twitter had taken its place among other social networking applications as the next big thing. But similar to MySpace and Facebook, it would experience growing pains.

WHO'S IN CHARGE?

In 2010, Twitter had approximately 15 million active users. The company had made approximately $25 million in revenue in 2009. It continued to operate on investment funds, having reportedly turned down an offer from Facebook to buy Twitter for $500 million.

Twitter invited outsiders—both individuals and companies—to create their own applications and services that would be featured on the site. Some created new "dashboards" for Twitter that made it easier for users to navigate the site. Others made it possible to link tweets with pictures or videos. Stone said, "There may be some 50 people officially working at Twitter, but it's more like 50,000 people work for Twitter, and they all deserve as much credit as we do."[1]

Twitter also introduced an application that allowed users to search through tweets for a current topic or specific subject—again, an application created by an outside company. Because this application turned out to be so successful, Twitter purchased Summize, the company that created the application, and hired most of its engineers.

Users themselves also created many of the features that have become standard on Twitter, such as replying, which allows the user to reply specifically to another user's tweet. However, when Twitter incorporated a user-generated feature that allowed users to share others' tweets by "retweeting" the same message as their own, Twitter did not make it possible for the retweeter to add a comment. This sparked protest from the users. Twitter was growing at a fast rate, but it needed to decide who was in charge: the users and the outside software developers, or Twitter itself. Up to that point, the company had

TWITTER IS WHAT YOU MAKE IT

In his interview with David Sarno of the *Los Angeles Times*, Dorsey notes that Twitter has never really changed from his original concept, proving that this unique form of communication works well and meets a need. He also points out that it is up to users to make Twitter work for them:

I've always said that Twitter is whatever you make of it. Because the first complaint we hear from everyone is: Why would I want to join this stupid useless thing and know what my brother's eating for lunch? But that really misses the point because Twitter is fundamentally recipient-controlled—you choose to listen and you choose to leave. But you also choose what to put down and what to share. So if you decide to hook your plants up to Twitter and have it report when it needs to be watered, then that's a valid usage, or if you just decide to report what you're eating for lunch, that's a valid usage too.[2]

focused mostly on maintaining its platform in a way that allowed for growth, but it had not made any innovations of its own.

Twitter also had to contend with an increasing amount of spam. Some companies utilized "twitomercials," which were repetitive tweets from dummy accounts about certain products or services. Some attempted to con people out of their money with offers of get-rich-quick schemes or messages from supposed family members who needed money. As Twitter became more popular, these types of spam were clogging the system. Many users felt that it was time for Twitter to take more control of its product for the benefit of users and the future of the company. Twitter began to limit applications created by outside software developers in order to create those applications itself, giving it more control as well as possibly attracting money from investors.

BUSINESS TWEETING

Twitter had also become a place for businesses and marketers to advertise. Companies such as Jet Blue airlines began using it as a place to market products, conduct market research, do promotions, and provide customer service. People could issue

a complaint about a company, and within a
few minutes they could receive a reply from the
company's representative about how the company
could help solve it.

As more companies joined Twitter, a rumor
developed that Twitter was going to start charging
brands a fee for using Twitter's service. Companies
threatened to leave the service, and regular users
wondered if they, too, would eventually be charged
to use Twitter. However, Twitter's founders assured
users that they had no intention of charging a user
fee. They said that any future revenue would come
from add-on services and not from charging for
existing services.

ARCHIVING TWITTER

In April 2010, an announcement by the Library
of Congress gave Twitter even more importance.
The library revealed that it would be archiving
every tweet posted since the site began in
March 2006. The Library of Congress believed that
the tweets, numbering in the billions, were important
parts of history that needed to be documented. Some
users expressed concern that their tweets were being
archived without their permission. However, director

of communications at the Library of Congress Matt Raymond assured users that the tweets would only be used for scholarly purposes. He pointed out that unless users had their account set as "private," the tweets were already available for public viewing in any case.

THE FUTURE OF TWITTER

Because of its openness in allowing outsiders to create applications for Twitter, the service has evolved more quickly than other social networking systems such as Facebook and MySpace. In the future, Twitter hopes to add even more new services to what it already has. According to Steven Levy:

Twitter envisions building its international audience by making deals with carriers to sell phones with Twitter connectivity built straight into the browser or texting functions. . . . The company also envisions delivering content from

ASHTON KUTCHER'S TWITTER RACE

One of Twitter's celebrity users is actor Ashton Kutcher. In 2009, Kutcher challenged the Cable News Network (CNN) to see who could acquire 1 million viewers to their Twitter account first. He beat CNN, attracting his millionth follower on April 17, 2009. The millionth person received a copy of the video game Guitar Hero from Kutcher, who also made a charitable contribution in honor of his win. "I found it astonishing that one person can actually have as big of a voice online as what an entire media company can on Twitter," Kutcher said.[3]

SAVED BY A TWEET

In April 2008, US journalism student James Karl Buck and his translator were arrested in Egypt after photographing antigovernment protests. On his way to the police station, the student used his cell phone to send the Twitter message "arrested" to his friends on Twitter. The friends alerted his university, the US Embassy in Cairo, and the press. The student was even able to send updates on his condition while he was in jail. The university hired a lawyer for him, and the student was released the next day.

Twitter to and from every connected device in your life, like radios and game consoles.[4]

Like any other social networking service that becomes wildly popular and then fades as users move on to the next new thing, Twitter will have to work to keep its popularity and grow as a company. But Twitter's advantage is that so many users are actively involved in helping the service grow. As Levy concludes, "The strength of Twitter is that the company already has thousands of people defining and redefining it every day."[5] +

Twitter's headquarters are located in San Francisco, California.

Barack Obama harnessed the power of social networking
for his presidential campaign.

SOCIAL NETWORKING AND SOCIETY

Social networking has quickly become a popular method of communication, especially among teenagers and young adults. While previous generations of teenagers relied mainly on the telephone as a way to stay in contact with their friends, today's teenagers can use cell phones, instant messaging, text messaging, and social networks online to maintain almost constant contact with their friends. But what are the positive and negative aspects of social networking, and how has it changed society?

LIMITLESS INTERACTION

One of the most exciting aspects of social networking is that it creates almost unlimited possibilities for meeting and interacting with people who might be outside the traditional boundaries of school, church, neighborhood, or workplace. It is easy to befriend people on a social networking site. This leads to connecting with friends of friends and creating circles of interaction well beyond the ways that traditional relationships are created. And because social networking sites are increasingly able to mimic face-to-face interaction better than e-mail or old-fashioned message boards, individuals can communicate more naturally.

Social networking sites are also ideal for quickly bringing together groups of people supporting a common cause. During his presidential campaign in 2008, Barack Obama's organization used Facebook

THE AGE STATISTICS

While people of all ages use the three major social networking sites, certain age groups tend to gravitate to certain sites. According to ages listed on personal profiles, the majority of MySpace users (34 percent) are teenagers. The highest number of Facebook users (27 percent) are in the 45 to 54 age group, as more adults find that Facebook is a good way to reconnect with old friends and classmates. Most Twitter users (29 percent) fall into the 35 to 44 age group, mostly due to the fact that many businesses utilize Twitter. However, there is no way to be sure of people's real ages on social networking sites because the sites do not verify this information when the user enters it.

and MySpace to organize local campaigns, raise money, respond to negative rumors, and gain support. As David Carr noted in the *New York Times*, "Obama understood that you could use the Web to lower the cost of building a political brand, [and] create a sense of connection and engagement."[1] Social networking has created a new way to unite users for a common cause or issue.

THE DARK SIDE

As social networking has become a bigger part of society, many negative aspects have also emerged. For teenagers, who are among the most avid users of social networking sites, electronic interaction has also allowed bullying to take place in an entirely new way. Harassing, insulting, and threatening can now take place online, 24 hours a day, 7 days a week. Too often, this cyberbullying leads to despair and even suicide among teenagers. A 15-year-old girl in Massachusetts killed herself in January 2010 after being a victim of vicious bullying both in person and via Facebook.

Another danger of social networking sites is that users never know for sure exactly who is viewing their personal information online. Some college admissions personnel routinely check online profiles when deciding whether to accept a prospective student. Many employers do the same thing when trying to decide whether to hire applicants.

Carolyn Axtell, a university researcher, notes, "Self-disclosure can indeed be a problem on the Internet. The fact that you can't see or hear other people makes it easier to reveal yourself in a way you might not be comfortable with."[2] A thoughtless post on a social networking site can result in a negative impression for anyone seeking information about that person, users, or subject.

Perhaps the darkest aspect of online social networking is the increased opportunity for sexual predators to find and exploit young victims. Although the dangers are often exaggerated in media reports, online predators still pose a risk to social networking users. Adult predators can create fake profiles. They can attempt to friend teenagers and entice them into meeting in person. According to the Netsmartz Web site of the National Center for Missing and Exploited Children, in a poll of teenagers who spend significant time online, 14 percent have met in person with someone they encountered on the Internet. Teens must be made aware that such meetings with strangers could lead to sexual assault or even murder.

Users of social networking sites—particularly adults—may also find their real-world relationships endangered by interaction with old friends and previous romantic interests. Reconnecting with a former love interest may incite jealousy in

FACEBOOK TEENS GROWING UP

A study done by the Pew Research Center in 2010 surveyed 895 technology experts and users for their opinions on how social networking would affect young people and their attitudes toward privacy as they grew into adulthood. Of those surveyed, 67 percent agreed with the following statement:

By 2020, members of Generation Y . . . will continue to be ambient broadcasters who disclose a great deal of personal information in order to stay connected and take advantage of social, economic, and political opportunities. Even as they mature, have families, and take on more significant responsibilities, their enthusiasm for widespread information sharing will carry forward.[3]

However, almost 30 percent disagreed with this statement. They felt that increased responsibilities and life changes as young people grew up would cause them to more carefully guard their private lives and share less personal information online.

a current partner and has even led to break-ups and divorces. According to writer Emma Justice, "Over a lifetime it's normal to lose touch with people as interests and circumstances change, but Facebook may alter the natural ebb and flow of friendship."[4]

THE FUTURE OF SOCIAL NETWORKING

As the popularity of both MySpace and Facebook levels off, some experts feel it indicates that many people are tired of social media. Even businesses that use social media sites as a way to advertise and solicit new contacts may return to traditional face-to-face interaction or print media. Most analysts feel that social networks may become more mobile but will continue to be important both socially and for business. Ram Shiram, a founding board member of Google, states, "Combining social and mobile—there is a new wave of opportunities coming up, a growth of users, so mobile Internet is clearly the next major computing cycle. Facebook will replace email for a new generation."[5]

Ultimately, social networking is about relationships and how they are sought and utilized. According to Lisa Hoover in a *PC World* article "How Social Networking Has Changed Society":

It's possible that these social networking tools are just the beginning of something, that they could lead to ways of finding and interacting with one another we never imagined, but whatever happens, you can't dismiss these tools easily. They are taking us somewhere exciting, but we have to work out how we deal with the fading boundaries these tools have left in their wake and that means rewriting our social rules as we go along.[6] +

Social networking sites have a large impact on
the lives of people around the world.

TIMELINE

1965	1970	1976
Chris DeWolfe is born in Portland, Oregon, in December.	Tom Anderson is born in Escondido, California, on November 8.	Jack Dorsey is born in St. Louis, Missouri, on November 19.

1999	2001	2002
LiveJournal is launched.	Chris DeWolfe and Tom Anderson meet while they are working at XDrive.	Friendster is launched.

1980s

1984

1997

Some computer users are already communicating using electronic bulletin boards.

Mark Zuckerberg is born in White Plains, New York, on May 14.

The first recognizable social network, SixDegrees.com, is launched.

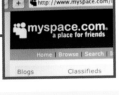

2003

2003

2004

MySpace is launched on August 15.

In October, Mark Zuckerberg creates the first version of Facebook, called Facemash, in his Harvard University dorm room.

Mark Zuckerberg and several other Harvard students launch Facebook on February 4.

TIMELINE

2004

2005

2006

The creators
of the Harvard
ConnectU site sue
Facebook and Mark
Zuckerberg on
September 2.

Rupert Murdoch's
company, News
Corporation, buys
MySpace in July.

The first version of
Twitter is launched
on March 21.

2009

2009

Chris DeWolfe steps
down as CEO
of MySpace.

Time magazine lists
the three founders
of Twitter among
the 100 Most
Influential People
in the World.

2007	2007	2008
In October, Microsoft pays $240 million for a share in Facebook.	Facebook launches Beacon on November 2, leading to widespread user protests about privacy.	A settlement is reached in the lawsuit against Facebook by ConnectU.

2010	2010	2010
Twitter has 15 million active users.	Facebook reaches more than 500 million active users.	*The Social Network*, a movie that tells the story of the founding of Facebook, is released in October.

ESSENTIAL FACTS

MYSPACE

Creators: Chris DeWolfe, December 1965
Tom Anderson, November 8, 1970

Date Launched: August 15, 2003

Challenges: MySpace's policy to quickly introduce new features often caused the site to crash. Additionally, many users complained of hackers, instances of pornography, and sexual predators on MySpace.

Successes: MySpace was the first popular social networking site in the United States. Unlike other sites, MySpace allowed people to create profiles for anything—including pets, companies, and bands.

FACEBOOK

Creator: Mark Zuckerberg, May 14, 1984

Date Launched: February 4, 2004

Challenges: Mark Zuckerberg dealt with several lawsuits against him. As Facebook grew popular, users sometimes disagreed with changes made to the site.

Successes: In October 2007, Microsoft made a $240 million investment in Facebook. As of 2010, Facebook was the most popular social networking site and one of the five most-visited Web sites in the world.

TWITTER

Creator: Jack Dorsey, November 19, 1976

Date Launched: March 21, 2006

Challenges: At first, Twitter was slow to gain popularity. Later on, Twitter faced a large amount of spam and get-rich-quick schemes that fooled some users into losing money.

Successes: In April 2010, the Library of Congress deemed all Twitter messages historically significant and began an archive of tweets. By 2010, Twitter had 15 million active users.

IMPACT ON SOCIETY

Social networking sites changed the way people communicated. They also created a platform for advertising and promotion of causes. However, the sites have also brought about concerns over privacy and protection from Internet predators.

QUOTE

"It's possible that these social networking tools are just the beginning of something, that they could lead to ways of finding and interacting with one another we never imagined . . ."—*Lisa Hoover*, PC World

GLOSSARY

analyst

Someone who is skilled at interpreting data or information on a certain topic and what it means in terms of marketing, trends, or popular culture.

blog

Short for *weblog;* an online journal or diary.

dispatch

To send something off or away with speed, such as a message or a service vehicle.

domain name

A name used in an Internet URL to identify a certain Web page or address, such as MySpace or Facebook.

entrepreneur

A person who creates and manages a new business, usually with some risk involved.

focus group

A small number of people brought together to be asked their opinions about a product, a service, an idea, or packaging for the purpose of market research.

jilted

Suddenly rejected or dropped from a relationship.

microchip

A small unit or package of computer circuitry for computer memory or logic, often made from silicon.

networking
A system of sharing information among groups with a common interest.

profile
A user's online page that contains his or her personal information.

programming language
A language, consisting of a specific computer-recognized code, used to write computer programs.

referral
Recommending or directing someone to a service, a product, or a specialist.

revenues
Income a company receives from its normal business activities.

spam
Unwanted and unsolicited electronic messages, usually advertising a product or a service.

unsolicited
Something that is not looked for, requested, or wanted.

URL
Uniform Resource Locator, the specific address of a Web page on the World Wide Web, such as www.facebook.com.

venture capital
Money made available to invest in a new business or enterprise.

ADDITIONAL RESOURCES

SELECTED BIBLIOGRAPHY

Angwin, Julia. *Stealing MySpace: The Battle to Control the Most Popular Website in America.* New York: Random House, 2009. Print.

Engdahl, Sylvia. *Current Controversies: Online Social Networking.* Farmington Hills, MI: Greenhaven Press, 2007. Print.

Mezrich, Ben. *The Accidental Billionaires: The Founding of Facebook.* New York: Doubleday, 2009. Print.

FURTHER READINGS

Jakubiak, David J. *A Smart Kid's Guide to Social Networking Online.* New York: Powerkids Press, 2009. Print.

Kuhn, Betsy. *Prying Eyes: Privacy in the Twenty-first Century.* Danbury, CT: Twenty-first Century Books, 2007. Print.

Stewart, Gail B. *Mark Zuckerberg: Facebook Creator.* Detroit, MI: KidHaven Press, 2009. Print.

WEB LINKS

To learn more about social networking, visit ABDO Publishing Company online at **www.abdopublishing.com**. Web sites about social networking are featured on our Book Links page. These links are routinely monitored and updated to provide the most current information available.

PLACES TO VISIT

Computer History Museum
1401 N. Shoreline Boulevard, Mountain View, CA 94043
650-810-1010
www.computerhistory.org
The Computer History Museum exhibits artifacts having to do with computers and the Internet. It focuses on the ways that computer technology has changed the world.

The Tech Museum
201 South Market Street, San Jose, CA 95113
408-294-8324
www.thetech.org
The Tech Museum has hundreds of exhibits relating to science and technology.

SOURCE NOTES

CHAPTER 1. THE WORLD OF SOCIAL NETWORKING

1. Christopher Nickson. "The History of Social Networking." *Digital Trends*. Digital Trends, 21 Jan. 2009. Web. 19 May 2010.

CHAPTER 2. FROM FINANCE AND FILM TO MYSPACE

1. "MySpace Cowboys: Chris DeWolfe." *CNNMoney.com*. Cable News Network, 4 Sept. 2006. Web. 19 May 2010.

2. Kevin Maney. "His Space." *Portfolio.com*. Bizjournals, 18 Mar. 2009. Web. 19 May 2010.

3. Evan Carmichael. "The Men Behind MySpace: How Chris DeWolfe and Tom Anderson First Met." *EvanCarmichael.com*. Evan Carmichael, n.d. Web. 19 May 2010.

4. Julia Angwin. *Stealing MySpace: The Battle to Control the Most Popular Website in America*. New York: Random House. 2009. Print. 14.

CHAPTER 3. CREATING MYSPACE

1. Kevin Maney. "His Space." *Portfolio.com*. Bizjournals, 18 Mar. 2009. Web. 19 May 2010.

2. Ibid.

3. Julia Angwin. *Stealing MySpace: The Battle to Control the Most Popular Website in America*. New York: Random House. 2009. Print. 22.

4. Evan Carmichael. "The Men Behind MySpace: How Chris DeWolfe and Tom Anderson First Met." *EvanCarmichael.com*. Evan Carmichael, n.d. Web. 19 May 2010.

5. Natalie Pace. "Q&A: MySpace Founders Chris DeWolfe and Tom Anderson." *Forbes.com*. Forbes.com, 4 Jan. 2006. Web. 19 May 2010.

6. Julia Angwin. *Stealing MySpace: The Battle to Control the Most Popular Website in America*. New York: Random House. 2009. Print. 7–8.

CHAPTER 4. MYSPACE MATURES

1. Julia Angwin. *Stealing MySpace: The Battle to Control the Most Popular Website in America*. New York: Random House. 2009. Print. 81.

2. Rebecca Hagelin. "Porn, Pedophiles, Our Kids, and MySpace. com." *Worldview Times*. Worldview Weekend.com, 29 May 2006. Web. 10 May 2010.

3. Joel Stein. "You Are Not My Friend." *Time*. Time, 4 Oct. 2007. Web. 19 May 2010.

4. Owen Gibson. "200 Million Friends and Counting." *Guardian. co.uk*. Guardian News and Media Limited, 23 Jun. 2008. Web. 19 May 2010.

CHAPTER 5. CONTROVERSIAL BEGINNINGS

1. Claire Hoffman. "The Battle for Facebook." *Rolling Stone*. Rolling Stone, 26 Jun. 2008. Web. 19 May 2010.

2. Katharine A. Kaplan. "Facemash Creator Survives Ad Board." *thecrimson.com*. Harvard Crimson, 19 Nov. 2003. Web. 19 May 2010.

3. Alan J. Tabak. "Harvard Bonds on Facebook Website." *thecrimson.com*. Harvard Crimson, 18 Feb. 2004. Web. 19 May 2010.

CHAPTER 6. FACEBOOK MOVES OFF CAMPUS

1. Claire Hoffman. "The Battle for Facebook." *Rolling Stone*. Rolling Stone, 26 Jun. 2008. Web. 19 May 2010.

2. Ibid.

3. Ibid.

4. "Facebook Must Respect Privacy." *MoveOn.org*. MoveOn.org Civic Action, 20 Nov. 2007. Web. 27 Jul. 2010.

5. Mark Zuckerberg. "Thoughts on Beacon." *Facebook*. Facebook, 5 Dec. 2007. Web. 19 May 2010.

SOURCE NOTES CONTINUED

CHAPTER 7. FACEBOOK ALL GROWN UP

1. Claire Hoffman. "The Battle for Facebook." *Rolling Stone.* Rolling Stone, 26 Jun. 2008. Web. 19 May 2010.

2. Ibid.

3. Brad Stone. "Is Facebook Growing Up Too Fast?" *New York Times.* New York Times, 28 Mar. 2009. Web. 19 May 2010.

4. Ibid.

5. Ibid.

6. Aaron Ricadela. "Fogeys Flock to Facebook." *Bloomberg Businessweek.* Bloomberg, 6 Aug. 2007. Web. 19 May 2010.

CHAPTER 8. HATCHING TWITTER

1. Josh Catone. "Award Winning Fiction in 140 Characters." *ReadWriteWeb.* ReadWriteWeb, 30 May 2008. Web. 16 Jun. 2010.

2. David Sarno. "Twitter Creator Jack Dorsey Illuminates the Site's Founding Document." *Los Angeles Times.* Los Angeles Times, 18 Feb. 2009. Web. 19 May 2010.

3. Ibid.

4. Dom Sagolla. "How Twitter Was Born." *140 Characters.* Dom Sagolla, 30 Jan. 2010. Web. 19 May 2010.

5. Ibid.

6. Andrew Lennon. "A Conversation with Twitter Cofounder Jack Dorsey." *The Daily Anchor.* The Daily Anchor, 12 Feb. 2009. Web. 19 May 2010.

CHAPTER 9. TWITTER TODAY

1. Steven Levy. "Who's in Charge?" *Wired.com.* Wired, 28 Sept. 2009. Web. 19 May 2010.

2. David Sarno. "Twitter Creator Jack Dorsey Illuminates the Site's Founding Document." *Los Angeles Times.* Los Angeles Times, 18 Feb. 2009. Web. 19 May 2010.

3. John D. Sutter. "CNN Retakes Lead in Twitter Battle with Ashton Kutcher." *CNNTech.* Cable News Network, 17 Apr. 2009. Web. 17 Aug. 2010.

4. Steven Levy. "Who's in Charge?" *Wired.com.* Wired, 28 Sept. 2009. Web. 19 May 2010.

5. Ibid.

CHAPTER 10. SOCIAL NETWORKING AND SOCIETY

1. David Carr. "How Obama Tapped Into Social Networks' Power." *New York Times.* New York Times, 9 Nov. 2008. Web.16 Jun. 2010.

2. Emma Justice. "'Facebook Suicide' Only Way Out for Some Web Addicts." *FoxNews.com.* FOX News Network, 27 Sept. 2007. Web. 16 Jun. 2010.

3. Janna Quitney Anderson and Lee Rainie. "Millennials Will Make Online Sharing in Networks a Lifelong Habit." *Pew Internet.* Pew Research Center, 9 Jul. 2010. Web. 27 Jul. 2010.

4. Emma Justice. "'Facebook Suicide' Only Way Out for Some Web Addicts." *FoxNews.com.* FOX News Network, 27 Sept. 2007. Web. 16 Jun. 2010.

5. Mercedes Bunz. "After Social Networks, What Next?" *Guardian. co.uk.* Guardian News and Media Limited, 24 Nov. 2009. Web. 16 Jun. 2010.

6. Lisa Hoover. "How Social Networking Has Changed Society." *PCWorld.* PCWorld Communications, 7 Apr. 2009. Web. 16 Jun. 2010.

INDEX

ABOUT THE AUTHOR

Marcia Amidon Lusted has written more than 40 books for young readers and more than 100 magazine articles. An assistant editor for Cobblestone Publishing, she also works as a writing instructor and musician. Lusted lives in New Hampshire with her family.

PHOTO CREDITS

Daniel Acker/Bloomberg via Getty Images, cover; Koji Sasahara/ AP Images, cover; Adrian Wyld/The Canadian Press/AP Images, 6; Jeff Adkins/News Sentinel/AP Images, 10; zetastock/Alamy, 13, 99 (bottom); Matt Sayles/AP Images, 14; Kevin Scanlon/Getty Images, 16; Jeff Vespa/WireImage/Getty Images, 21, 96; Erik Freeland/ Corbis, 22, 97 (bottom); Andrew Goetz/Corbis, 31; Richard Drew/ AP Images, 32; Mike Derer/AP Images, 37; Brad Barket/MySpace/ AP Images, 41; Paul Sakuma/AP Images, 42, 97 (top); Juana Arias/ The Washington Post/Getty Images, 49, 99 (top); Kimberly White/ Getty Images, 50; Charles Krupa/AP Images, 57; Alex Wong/ Getty Images, 59; Gilles Mingasson/Getty Images, 60; Ramin Talaie/Bloomberg via Getty Images, 65; Paul Sakuma/AP Images, 69; Khalid Mohammed/AP Images, 70; Jeff Chiu/AP Images, 73; Mike Kepka/San Francisco Chronicle/Corbis, 79; Jemal Countess/ WireImage for Time Inc., 80, 98; David Paul Morris/Getty Images, 87; Frank Micelotta/Getty Images, 88; AP Images, 95